What Is an **Athlete?**

To Doug and Scott—B.L.
To Andy—C.K.

Published by The Millbrook Press, Inc.
2 Old New Milford Road
Brookfield, CT 06804
www.millbrookpress.com

Library of Congress Cataloging-in-Publication Data
Lehn, Barbara.
What is an athlete? / Barbara Lehn ; photographs by Carol Krauss.
p. cm.
Summary: Simple text and photographs depict young people engaged in
activities that embody the qualities of an athlete.
ISBN 0-7613-2258-2 (lib. bdg.)
1. Athletes—Juvenile literature. 2. Athletics—Vocational
guidance—Juvenile literature. [1. Athletes. 2. Occupations.]
I.Krauss, Carol, ill. II. Title.
GV705.4 .L45 2002
796'.023'73—dc21 2001007592

Special thanks to all the children, families, and organizations who
contributed to this book including Merritting Attention, Inc., Ironstone Farms,
LA Rock Gym, Zephyr Aquatic Club, and the Skating Academy.

What Is an Athlete?

Barbara Lehn
Photographs by Carol Krauss

The Millbrook Press
Brookfield, Connecticut

An athlete is **determined** to do her physical best.

Jackie puts everything she has into her game.

"I know I can pass the ball to Carly if I just keep it in control," thinks Jackie.

An athlete **develops skills** over time with practice.

Joey practices riding the quarter bowl.

"I'm trying to keep my balance, but I need more practice," says Joey.

An athlete has **strength** and **grace**.

Jazzy plays basketball one-on-one with Julian.

Jazzy says, "Sometimes I feel like I could fly when I lift off to shoot a basket."

An athlete
exercises
self-control
and **focus**.

Giancarlo concentrates on his next pitch as he winds up.

Giancarlo plans, "I'm going to fire this one right down the middle."

An athlete **makes** split-second **decisions**.

Caitlene learns where her hands need to be on the uneven bars.

"If I can't make the grab this way, I'll need to go into my finish," decides Caitlene.

An athlete **learns** from experience.

Summer practices her backhand during a tennis lesson.

"My shot is going to be too high because I didn't turn my racket," thinks Summer.

An athlete is
someone who
trusts himself
to perform well.

Rowland skies downhill after his lesson.

Rowland says, "It's really fun to come blasting down the hill, but I know how to slow down when I need to."

An athlete is a **risk taker**.

Austin is proud of the stunts he can do on horseback.

"I was right. I can lie down facing backward!" exclaims Austin.

An athlete uses the right equipment for **safety**.

Alyssa climbs the rock wall in gym class.

Alyssa says, "When I'm on belay, the ropes and harness have to be on correctly in case I fall."

An athlete **eats well** in order to play well.

Sarah and Annie enjoy a snack before they go to hockey practice.

"It's important to eat right so we have plenty of energy to play," says Sarah.

An athlete communicates and **cooperates** with teammates.

Ernie moves in so Henry can pass the ball to him.

"I'm right here, Henry. Pass it over to me!" calls Ernie.

An athlete **respects** and **appreciates** his opponents.

Nick appreciates Scott's ability as a swimmer.

"I know Scott will probably always beat me, but I like to race him. I always swim faster against Scott," admits Nick.

An athlete has **fun**!

Pastor has discovered a new passion.

"I just started skating six months ago and I LOVE IT!" declares Pastor.

An athlete is a person who . . .

does her best

practices skills

has strength
and grace

focuses on the
game

makes quick
decisions

learns from
experience

trusts himself

is a risk taker

uses safety gear

respects opponents

eats well

cooperates with
teammates

has fun!

That's
what an
athlete
is!

About the **Author** and **Photographer**

Barbara Lehn has been involved in regular and special education for more than 25 years. She currently teaches first grade in Concord, Massachusetts, where she continually learns from her students. Barbara lives in Andover, Massachusetts, with her husband and their son.

Carol Krauss turned to professional photography after a career in management consulting. Her black and white fine art prints can be seen at a variety of New England galleries. She also does freelance photography for individuals and businesses in the area. She has collaborated with her friend Barbara Lehn on two other books—WHAT IS A SCIENTIST?, and WHAT IS A TEACHER? Carol lives in Concord, Massachusetts with her family and dog.